PADI®
Night Diver
Manual

Improve Your Scuba

PADI®
Night Diver
Manual

Published by PADI
P.O. Box 25011
Santa Ana, CA 92799-5011

Library of Congress Card Number 94-078001
ISBN 1-878663-14-3

Printed in the United States of America
10 9 8 7 6 5 4 3

PRODUCT NO. 79301

Table of Contents

Reacting to light, an octopus jets away into the blackness.

Introduction

Like a brush on black canvas, your light sweeps across the night reef, igniting a vibrant spectrum that somehow eluded you during the day. You pause, amazed by nature's endless pallette; everywhere your light falls new hues burst forth.

Your buddy waves his light to get your attention, then points as an octopus crawls amid the reef. During the day octopus hide, but at night emerge, protected by darkness. Reacting to your light, it freezes a moment, changes colors, then jets away into the blackness. Your buddy smiles behind his mask; these are just some of the rewards of night diving.

Most divers find night diving mysterious, yet alluring. At night, the familiar dive site takes on a new aura and new adventure. Darkness lays a veil you penetrate with your lights as you explore. Even the flora and fauna differ as underwater life switches to nocturnal behaviors, and as nocturnal animals emerge.

The PADI Night Diver Specialty expands your knowledge of night diving procedures.

While night diving sounds eerie, perhaps even a bit frightening to some divers, for others it's the first specialty activity they try. Night diving isn't difficult, and a few guidelines and procedures make night diving even more fun and safe. The PADI Night Diver Specialty course and the PADI Advanced Open Water core night dive both teach you these procedures and let you practice them with a PADI Instructor at hand.

Course Overview

The PADI Night Diver Specialty course is divided into knowledge development and open water training. In addition, your PADI Instructor may add confined water (pool) and other sessions, depending upon your location and the needs of the class.

The knowledge development portion expands your knowledge about night diving equipment, evaluating dive conditions at night, using and maintaining dive lights, night navigation, aquatic life and other topics. Knowledge development is usually accomplished through independent study with the PADI *Night Diving* video, this manual and other references, followed by predive review and discussion with your instructor. At your instructor's discretion, more formal classroom sessions may be held.

Understanding night diving procedures forms the basis for *applying them*, which you master during open water training. You'll make at least three night dives accompanied by your instructor, practicing and demonstrating the practical aspects of diving at night. You'll have fun practicing what you learn in this manual and by watching *Night Diving*.

When you successfully complete the course, you'll be awarded the PADI Night Diver certification. Earning this certification means that you're qualified to plan, organize and make night dives in conditions similar to those you train in.

When you successfully complete the course, you'll be awarded the PADI Night Diver certification.

PADI Specialty Diver Course
and Advanced Open Water Program Relationship

Each dive in your PADI Advanced Open Water Diver or Advanced Plus course is the first dive from a corresponding PADI Specialty Diver course. These specialties include: Altitude Diver, Boat Diver, Deep Diver, Drift Diver, Dry Suit Diver, Multilevel Diver, Peak Performance Buoyancy, Underwater Navigator, Night Diver, Search and Recovery Diver, Underwater Naturalist, Underwater Photographer and Wreck Diver. If you've already earned a PADI Advanced Open Water or Advanced Plus certification, a dive may be applied, at your instructor's discretion, to the appropriate specialty course. Likewise, if you're not yet a PADI Advanced Open Water or Advanced Plus Diver, the first dive you make in a specialty course may be credited, at your instructor's discretion, to your Advanced Open Water program.

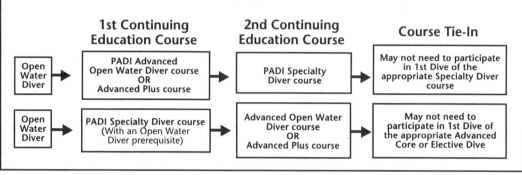

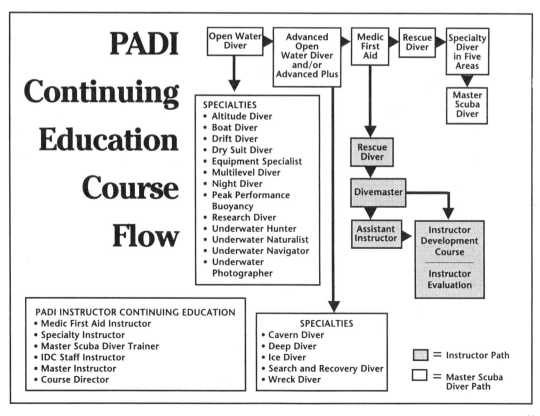

PADI Continuing Education Course Flow

Getting the Most from the PADI *Night Diving* Video

The companion video to this manual is *Night Diving*, which shows you what you'll practice and experience during your training dives. Combining video, manual and open water training is the most effective way to learn, *retain* and review diving knowledge and skills. You'll find learning easiest by following these steps with *Night Diving* and the PADI *Night Diver Manual:*

1. Watch *Night Diving*. This gives you the basic concepts of what you'll be learning. This award winning video is entertaining as well as educational, so relax and enjoy yourself as you watch.

2. Read this manual, following the instructions in "How to Use This Book." Be sure to underline/highlight, answer exercises and complete the Knowledge Reviews. As you do so, you'll learn the theory and detail of night diving.

3. Just before your training dives, watch *Night Diving* again. Since you'll have completed reading this manual by then, you'll comprehend more detail as you watch, and what you've learned will be refreshed and reinforced.

4. After you've completed the course, review this manual and watch *Night Diving* periodically to keep your skills and knowledge intact, especially when it's been a while since you've made night dives. Also, use the Night Diving Log Insert (included with the video) when you dive as a handy equipment/technique reference.

How to Use This Book

The PADI *Night Diver Manual* is an interactive book designed to assist you in remembering the material you read. Use the following guidelines to maximize your learning.

First, find a quiet, comfortable study environment. Next, begin by *previewing* an individual section. Effective previewing means skimming the section quickly, reading italicized or highlighted words, subheadings and captions.

After previewing the section, return to its beginning. You'll notice that each section has a set of Study Objectives stated as questions. Read these carefully, before concentrating on the section. The questions will guide your learning.

Now, read each section looking for answers to the Study Objective questions. Underline or highlight answers as you find them.

Immediately after you've finished reading a

section, return to the beginning and review your underlined or highlighted answers. Make sure you have underlined or highlighted an answer for each Study Objective question.

At the end of each section, you'll find an exercise with questions to answer. These exercises allow you assess your comprehension quickly and effectively. The exercises ask you to mark an immediate response directly in your book. Once you choose an answer, compare it with the correct one provided. If your answer was incorrect, reread the related material plus your underlined or highlighted response within the section.

Finally, at the end of the book, you'll find a Knowledge Review. Your instructor will ask you to complete the Knowledge Review and turn it in to him. Before your training dives, your instructor will review it with you.

By the time you complete the Knowledge Review, you should be thoroughly familiar with the material in the book. However, if you find there's something you "just can't get," despite rereading the material, be sure to have your instructor explain it to you. Remember, your instructor's first concern is that you have a safe and fun experience on each dive. Understanding and remembering the information in this book is part of the process.

Watch for These Symbols

As you read the *Night Diver Manual*, you'll notice these symbols:

 Alerts you to important safety information. Pay close attention when you see this symbol and consult your instructor if you do not understand the material.

 This Project A.W.A.R.E. symbol highlights information or a specific diving technique that allows you to harmoniously interact with the aquatic environment.

 Alerts you to additional sources of information and topics covered in PADI videos.

 MFA This symbol highlights information that you can become familiar with in the PADI Medic First Aid course.

 Alerts you to additional sources of information for deeper and/or broader topic coverage. This symbol is for your interest and further reading; all information necessary for safe and enjoyable training dives will be covered in the *Night Diver Manual*.

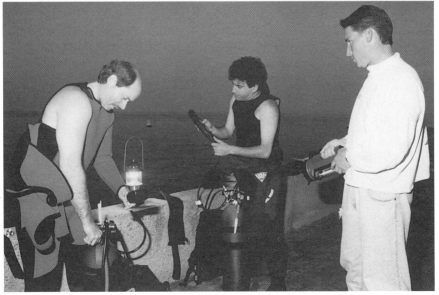

Study Objectives

Underline/highlight the answers to these questions as you read:

1. What are five reasons for night diving?

2. What three diving specialty activities benefit from night diving?

Why Dive at Night?

Since you're reading this book, it's reasonable to assume that you want to night dive and know why. However, it helps to understand some motivations other divers may have so your buddies *and* you get what you want out of night diving. You can split these motivations into five general categories.

The first is natural curiosity. To many divers, a night dive spells adventure and a chance to explore the unknown. They hope to discover things they wouldn't during the day, or they may be attracted by the added challenge darkness brings to diving.

Aquatic life provides a second reason for night diving. At sunset, animals active during the day retire, and night creatures emerge. In salt and fresh water, many fish seek shelter in the reef; some change color as they "sleep" on the bottom. Nocturnal fish and other animals, such as catfish and lobster, become active at night. By diving at night, you encounter a new set of organisms, and a new set of behaviors.

Third, because the underwater world at night differs from day, many divers enjoy night diving to get a new look at familiar dive sites. Besides different aquatic life, night adds a new dimension, so that the same old reef or wreck appears fresh and different.

Some fish "sleep" on the bottom at night.

Many divers enjoy night diving to get a new look at a familiar dive site – that same old wreck appears fresh and different.

1

A fourth reason is that many divers enjoy the vibrant colors that characterize a night dive. As you learned in your entry-level course, water absorbs color from light passing through it. Water absorbs red first, then orange, followed by yellow and green a good bit deeper, leaving only blue (in clear water). During the day, this absorption filters the sunlight, muting the colors you see. At night, you see by your dive light close at hand; its light doesn't travel through much water, so colors remain bright and true.

Finally, you'll encounter many people who night dive because it gives them more chances to dive. Hectic work schedules and office hours restrict many divers' diving to weekends – unless they night dive. During the week, such individuals can enjoy night dives after working hours. Likewise, on a dive trip night diving gets in one more dive at the end of the day.

Night Diving Activities

You can enjoy most specialty diving activities at night, just as you do during the day. However, night diving particularly enhances three specialties – Underwater Naturalist, Underwater Photographer/ Videographer and Wreck Diver.

As mentioned, aquatic organisms behave differently at night. This presents the underwater naturalist with more opportunities to observe unique creatures and unique behaviors. Whether you're watching a cone shell glide across sand or a carp rutting through the mud, night diving expands your familiarity with underwater life (more about nocturnal aquatic life in the next section).

Underwater photographers/videographers enjoy night diving because they can photo/video nocturnal flora and fauna. Organisms that become dormant – especially fish – can be approached easily for close ups that would be difficult or impossible during the day. To some videographers and photographers, night provides a dramatic backdrop against which to contrast vivid underwater colors.

Wreck diving also benefits from night diving.

Night diving presents opportunities to observe unique creatures, like a cone shell gliding across sand.

The night environment provides a dramatic backdrop for underwater pictures.

Many divers enjoy wrecks because they can seem mystic and adventurous. At night, largely intact wrecks become ghostlike, adding to the adventure and mystery.

An important point: Wreck penetrations should not be made at night. If you're qualified to penetrate overhead environments, do so only during the day; be content to look in the ports and windows at night.

Approaching fish for closeup photographs is easier at night than during the day.

Night Diving and Overhead Environments

Any environment that prohibits a direct vertical ascent to the surface is regarded as an overhead environment. These include caves, caverns, inside wrecks or under ice. As you're probably aware, overhead environments require specialized equipment, techniques and training. However, even with these, recreational diving precludes venturing into overhead environments at night. Recreational divers in overhead environments always re-main within sight of daylight. This provides another way to locate the exit in case of light failure, disorientation, and contact loss with the guideline. Night dives rule out this primary safety advantage; therefore, it's inappropriate to make overhead environment dives at night. To learn more about proper techniques for overhead environments, enroll in the PADI Wreck Diver, Cavern Diver or Ice Diver Specialty courses.

Objectives

Underline/highlight the answers to these questions as you read:

1. What are three commonly observed types of nocturnal aquatic life found in salt water? In fresh water?

2. What are four behaviors that aquatic life displays at night?

3. How should you interact responsibly with nocturnal aquatic life?

Nocturnal Aquatic Life

Whether you're diving in a lake or the ocean, in warm water or cool, and at a high latitude or near the equator, aquatic life changes with nightfall. As mentioned earlier, at dark some creatures retire while others come out of hiding. Some change behavior.

The varieties of nocturnal organisms and their individual behaviors would take volumes to fill. Nonetheless, you'll find a few creatures routinely in salt water and fresh water. Also, you'll encounter several unique behaviors on a routine basis, most of which involve reproduction or feeding.

Saltwater Aquatic Life

With their greater variety of life, oceans and seas abound with interesting creatures at night. As mentioned before, it's a real treat to encounter an octopus, which is common in both tropical and temperate water.

During the day, the octopus stays hidden in a crevice or hole, but at night it roams about searching for food. Considered one of the most intelligent invertebrates, the octopus reacts strongly to being shined on with dive lights. Typically, it freezes and changes colors, trying to blend in with the reef.

Considered one of the most intelligent invertebrates, the octopus reacts strongly to being shined on with dive lights.

You can look for lobster all day and never spot one, only to have one walk by at night.

When that doesn't work, it may try to crawl or jet away, or it may advance toward the light.

If you spot an octopus, avoid shining your light directly on it. Instead, use the edge of your light beam to watch it. This way, you're less likely to frighten it and more likely to see it behave normally. Besides the octopus, don't be surprised if you run into its nocturnal cousins: the squid and the cuttlefish.

Crustaceans – shrimp, lobster and crabs – are the octopus' favorite food, and also a common sight on night dives. Like the octopus, crustaceans tend to be elusive in the day, but wander around scavenging by night. You can look for lobster all day and never spot one, only to have several walk by on a night dive.

Most crustaceans don't shy away from light as much as octopus do. In fact, you'll often first spot shrimp by reflection from their eyes. There's hundreds of shrimp species in amazing variety, so look closely. You may be surprised by what you find.

Another interesting crustacean is the hermit crab, known for living in shells it finds. If you find several in the same area, sit back and watch quietly. You may catch them scurrying about trading shells and picking up new ones.

During the day you usually find eels with their heads poking from their holes, but at night, they

You may catch sight of hermit crabs scurring about trading shells.

This zebra moray appears snake-like as it undulates along the bottom. It's actually a fish.

often come out and swim freely. They appear somewhat snakelike as they undulate their way

Many shells wait until dark before showing themselves.

along the bottom, but actually they're fish. Depending upon your location, you may encounter moray, conger, monkey face or wolf eels.

Besides highly active creatures like octopi, crustaceans and eels, less active animals come out at night. Many shells (actually mollusks) wait under the sand until dark, then show themselves, gliding slowly across the bottom. Look for them in sandy areas that seem barren by day. You only find Spanish dancers and several other nudibranch species at night, too. Brittle stars, basket stars, crinoids, sea stars and other invertebrates that you run into during the day come more into the open at night.

Some species of nudibranchs, like this Spanish Dancer, only come out at night.

Freshwater Aquatic Life

In fresh water, you'll encounter many of the same types of creatures, but not necessarily in the same variety or abundance. This includes the freshwater version of lobster – the crayfish (also called crawfish or crawdad). Like its saltwater brethren, the crayfish tends to be reclusive by day, but comes out to scavenge by night. Like shrimp, you'll find that their eyes often give them away.

Another nocturnal freshwater denizen is the catfish. At night, catfish become active, and rut through the bottom scavenging for food. Catfish are put off by light a bit, but not enough to keep you from watching as they skim through the sediment with their barbels.

Like catfish, carp also feed at night. They, too, comb the bottom for food, but tend to freeze when you put your light on them.

Eels inhabit some freshwater environments, especially springs. Like saltwater eels, these fish become active at night and emerge from their daytime hiding places. You may see no eels at all

Bioluminescence

On some night dives, you'll find that swiftly waving your hand produces "sparks" – bursts of light like tiny fireflies. You may notice a glowing trail behind you as you swim, or that boat propeller wash luminesces distinctly.

What you're observing is bioluminescence – the ability of some marine organisms to generate light chemically. Although most bioluminescent organisms live hundreds of feet/metres deep, quite a few exist in the shallows, too.

As a night diver, you'll most commonly encounter bioluminescent zooplankton called *dinoflagellates*. Dinoflagellates are microscopic, but when agitated (such as by your hand, fin or a boat prop), they emit a bright momentary glow. When these plankton are dense, this can result in a steady stream of sparkling light from anything that moves in the water.

during a day dive in a relatively small spring, for example, and be amazed at how many come out after dark. Because freshwater eels look even more snakelike than their saltwater counterparts, some people experience anxiety when they encounter one. It helps to remember that they're fish.

Nocturnal Behavior

In addition to seeing animals at night that you don't during the day, you'll also see different behavior from creatures you encounter routinely during the day. In tropical settings, coral sets perhaps the most conspicuous example.

During the day, coral appears hard and stonelike, but after dark, the coral polyps open and extend to feed on plankton. As a result, coral heads look soft and velvety, as if covered by a blanket of fuzz. Coral feeding behavior vividly demonstrates that it is both alive and delicate; because you can easily injure the open polyps,

After dark, coral polyps open to feed on plankton. As a result, coral heads look soft and velvety.

exercise caution to avoid touching the coral.

Common freshwater and saltwater fish "sleep" at night. They either rest on the bottom or glide as

Usually your light won't bother sleeping fish, making it easy to get a close look.

if in a trance, and some species change color or become pale. Usually your light won't bother sleeping fish, making it easy to get a close look or take a picture. This provides opportunities to photograph species that you can't approach during the day.

Although sleeping fish usually react little to lights, some react strongly to the lightest touch. Often they bolt away in any direction, running into divers or the reef, oblivious to injuries they inflict on themselves. With this in mind, you'll want to be cautious to avoid touching them.

One tropical fish, the parrot fish, takes an unusual step to ensure it won't be bothered while it rests. It secretes a mucous sack that envelopes it, rather like a bubble. Look for sleeping parrot fish under ledges and other sheltered spots.

Your dive light may attract some organisms, including plankton, small crustaceans and worms that swarm around dive lights. These in turn may attract fish, thickening the crowd around your light.

In some areas, jellyfish, including stinging sea wasps, migrate toward light (more on this later). Local dive guides can tell you which organisms may be drawn to light, and techniques for avoiding them.

Because each environment has distinct nocturnal life, your PADI Instructor will discuss specific aquatic life and unique behaviors that you may encounter during your PADI Night Diver Specialty course training dives or Advanced core night dive.

The parrot fish secretes a mucous sack that envelopes it like a bubble to ensure it won't be bothered while it rests.

Interacting with Aquatic Life

As a certified diver, you probably have a strong awareness of your responsibility in interacting with aquatic life. This includes taking steps to avoid inadvertent injury or damage to the organisms you encounter.

At night, you need to be extra vigilant to maintain this commitment. With visibility limited to your light beam, you have to work harder to avoid bumping into things. At the same time, many organisms are more exposed, and therefore more prone to injury.

Considering how sleeping fish may react when

touched, avoid doing so, intentionally or accidentally. Be aware that your light can cause harm, too,

Consider how a sleeping fish may react when touched; avoid doing so intentionally or accidentally.

if you use it to push or prod. In fact, it may be more harmful than if you used your hand.

Interact by moving cautiously and slowly. Maintain neutral buoyancy. Give animals the option to approach, remain where they are or retreat. You may find that a snail or nudibranch readily crawls onto your palm, but an octopus will be timid. Other creatures, such as squid, may appear curious and won't run from you, provided they don't feel cornered or threatened. When in doubt, don't touch aquatic animals at all; this prevents injury to either you or the animal.

By moving slowly with care, you're less likely to harm or significantly alarm the aquatic life you meet. In return, you'll be rewarded by seeing more aquatic life behaving naturally.

When You Meet Mantas

Few nocturnal encounters thrill divers as much as those with manta rays. In Hawaii, Yap and other Pacific locations, manta come inshore to feed on plankton attracted by shore lights. This makes close interaction with mantas possible.

The key to having a manta swim over your head, nearly at snorkel level, is to hold still and point your light up. The beam attracts plankton, which in turn attracts the mantas.

As long as you hold still, the rays will glide through your beam, mouths open, to eat the plankton. It's a truly memorable experience to have these giant rays swim just above you.

· **Exercise 2** **Nocturnal Aquatic Life**

1. Commonly encountered nocturnal animals in the ocean include (check all that apply):
   ☐ a. octopus ☐ b. crustaceans ☐ c. eels ☐ d. damsel fish
2. Unique aquatic life nocturnal behaviors include (check all that apply):
   ☐ a. extended coral polyps ☐ b. sleeping fish ☐ c. parrot fish feeding on coral
3. Responsible interaction with aquatic life at night ☐ a. differs little from interaction during
   the day. ☐ b. requires extra care

How did you do?
1. a,b, c. Damsel fish may be present, but they are not nocturnal and tend to remain motionless at night. 2. a,b. Parrot fish usually envelope themselves in a mucous bubble at night. 3. b.

Study Objectives

Underline/highlight the answers to these questions as you read:

1. What personal dive equipment considerations does a night dive require?

2. What is the recommendation regarding the use of new or unfamiliar equipment at night?

Night Diving Equipment

With the exception of lights (to which the entire next section is devoted), there's little difference between the equipment you use during the day and the equipment you use at night. Rather, equipment

With the exception of lights, there's little difference between the equipment you use during the day and during the night.

placement and operation become primary considerations because it's harder to see at night and you have a light in one hand. Generally speaking, you'll

It's hard to see your alternate air source at night, making it important to keep it positioned in the triangle formed by your chin and the lower corners of your rib cage where it's easy to find and secure.

be more comfortable if you can locate each piece by touch, and if you can work it with one hand.

This especially applies to your alternate air source, which should be easily accessible in an emergency. Regardless of type, ideally, clearly mark it with a contrasting color for easy identification by your buddy in the dark. Mount it with a quick release holder on your chest in the triangle formed by your chin and the corners of your rib cage. This ensures you can find it easily, and that it doesn't drag and fill with mud or sand.

Be sure you can find your BCD low pressure inflator easily. Most popular models stay put pretty well, but if yours has a tendency to float or swing behind your shoulder, you may want to use velcro or a retaining strap to keep it in place. Of course, this should be done in a way that doesn't interfere with using it – see your PADI Dive Center about options for securing the inflator.

You're more likely to brush into things in the dark, so it's a good idea to wear an exposure suit, even if you don't need one to keep warm. Likewise, consider wearing gloves and wet suit boots to protect your hands and ankles. Since night diving tends to be cooler than day diving, you may want thermal protection, too, even though you didn't during the day. A wet, dry or skin suit helps avoid scrapes and stings; just keep in mind that you're protected from aquatic life, but it's not protected from you. When thinking about exposure protection, don't forget before and after the dive; if nights are cool, bring a suitable jacket or coat.

Many divers find instrument consoles especially convenient for night dives. Consoles make it easy to check your SPG, depth gauge and timer/computer, and other gauges in a single glance. Many gauges glow in the dark, so you don't need to use your light to read them; others light electronically, and some consoles have a place for chemical light sticks to illuminate your gauges.

Night diving communication relies primarily on hand signals, just like during the day (more on this later), but you'll find a slate extra useful for signals that aren't as effective at night. For instance, you may see something you want to alert your buddy to,

Many divers find instrument consoles convenient. Some gauges will glow in the dark after being exposed to light.

Shriekers, Shiners and Sausages

While most divers carry whistles as their primary alert signals, you have options. These include shriekers (noise makers), shiners (flashers and strobes) and sausages (inflatable signal tubes).

Shriekers include battery-operated units that wail or siren loud enough to penetrate wind and engine noise. Many of these work underwater as well as at the surface. Air-powered devices attach in line between the low pressure inflator hose and the inflator itself; you use these only at the surface. Manufacturers caution that these are very loud and should be held well away from your ears.

Because shriekers rely on either batteries or having air in your tank, it's recommended that you still carry your trusty whistle, which requires neither.

Visual signals (shiners) include small, high intensity strobe lights and special mirrors from which you can reflect your dive light or a search light. Inflatable signal tubes (sausages) unroll and inflate to jut well above the surface. These are much easier to spot than a diver's head, and you can make them even more visible at night by shining your light on or up through them. Rolled up, inflatable signal tubes are about the size of a roll of coins, and fit easily in your BCD pocket.

Alert signals can include noise makers, flashers and strobes, and inflatable signal tubes.

A whistle or other audible device is important so you can communicate at the surface from a distance.

but it's beyond light range, or you don't know exactly where it is in the dark. You can't point to it as you would during the day, so writing is more effective than signaling and pointing.

A whistle or other audible device is important so you can communicate at the surface with the boat or shore from a distance. If a buddy team were caught down current, for example, they'd whistle to alert the crew. Most divers secure their whistle to their BCD hose near the inflator, so they can find and use it easily.

It's not a bad idea to carry visual signaling devices, too. These make it easier for the boat to spot you, or for your buddy to relocate you if you become separated and need to regroup on the surface.

The general recommendation is that for night dives, use equipment with which you're familiar and comfortable. If you're using unfamiliar equipment that requires a change in procedures or placement, it's a good idea to get used to it during the day, first.

Obviously, you don't have to think about where to find or how to use a snorkel, even if it's brand new. On the other hand, you may not be able to use a new BCD or regulator configuration instinctively until you've made a couple dives with it. By getting used to these and making any adjustments during the day, you'll make your night dives more relaxing and comfortable.

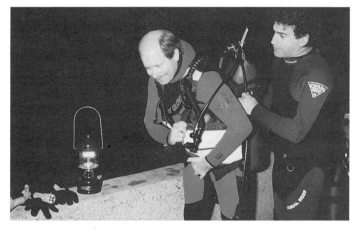

The general recommendation is to use equipment with which you're familiar and comfortable.

Exercise 3

Night Diving Equipment

1. Which of the following equipment has some considerations for use at night (check all that apply)? ☐ a. alternate air source ☐ b. weight belt ☐ c. BCD inflator ☐ d. mask

2. The general recommendation for using new or unfamiliar equipment is

☐ a. to use it at night immediately so you become comfortable with it in the dark quickly.

☐ b. to first use it during the day to become familiar with it.

How did you do?
1. a,c.   2. b.

Study Objectives

Underline/highlight the answers to these questions as you read:

1. Why is it important to carry at least two lights on a night dive?

2. What six features should you look for in a dive light?

3. Why should some dive lights only be switched on underwater?

4. What are the advantages and disadvantages of rechargeable and nonrechargeable batteries for dive lights?

Underwater Light Systems

When you first decided to try night diving, one of the first things you probably thought was "I need a dive light." Few divers would seriously consider trying to navigate, read gauges, communicate with their buddies and sightsee at night without one.

However, you may not be aware that compared to other dive equipment like BCDs and regulators, dive lights aren't as consistently reliable. This isn't the fault of light manufacturers – it's the nature of all lights – bulbs burn out and batteries go dead on dive lights just like on regular lights. Further complicating the problem, an improperly maintained dive light can flood and fail.

Without a light, in clear water under a bright moon, you can see surprisingly well, but not so well that you'd want to surface and exit the water without a light if you can avoid it. Under less ideal conditions and no moon, you can't see that much.

When you night dive, you need not one, but at least two dive lights: a primary and a backup.

So, when you night dive, you need not one, but at least two dive lights: a primary and a backup. Actually, many divers carry two or more backup lights for added confidence that they won't have to surface without one.

Most divers select a large, primary light that they carry and use unless it fails. Backup lights tend to be more compact, slipped into the BCD

Backup lights are often slipped into a BCD pocket or clipped to a D-ring.

pocket or clipped to a D ring, where it won't entangle other equipment or bash against the reef. During your predive safety check, you and your buddy should familiarize each other with where you keep your backups.

Dive Light Features 📖

When you visit your dive store to select a dive light, you may be surprised at the variety you can choose from. They range from large primary lights, to compact backups, to specialized lights like video lights. No matter what the purpose, look for these six features when you buy a dive light:

Dive lights range from large primary lights to compact backups.

Rugged Case

To prevent corrosion, dive lights are made primarily from aluminum or, most commonly, plastic. They need to be strong enough to withstand pressure, and tough enough to endure rough handling and the occasional bump or drop.

Fortunately, modern manufacturers construct dive lights lights with this in mind, so most of them stand up to the abuses of normal diving easily. Common materials include ABS plastic and polycarbonate (also called "Lexan"). ABS is impact and UV resistant; polycarbonate is a clear, impact resistant plastic commonly used for lens (and underwater housings).

Dependable switches

You'll find several types of switches on dive lights. These include magnetic switches, screw down lenses, O-ring gland switches and rubber boot covered switches. Each of these works well, with advantages and disadvantages.

Magnetic switches have the advantage of not penetrating the case, thereby eliminating a potential leak. However, they can become temperamental with wear. Screw down lenses also eliminate an extra case penetration, but if you're not careful, such lights will turn on by themselves when you descend and water pressure pushes in on the lens.

A nice feature on any light is a switch lock that ensures the light stays off in your gear bag.

Both O-ring gland and rubber boot switches penetrate the light case. O-ring gland switches are very reliable, positive switches, but need proper maintenance so they don't leak. O-ring gland switches should be rinsed very thoroughly and may require periodic lubrication (consult manufacturer guidelines).

Rubber boots wear out over time and must be replaced to prevent leakage. You'll find them primarily on older lights; manufacturers don't use them much any more.

A nice feature on any dive light is a switch lock that ensures the light stays off in your gear bag, without removing the batteries.

O-ring seals

A dive light must have at least one watertight O-ring sealed opening that gives you access to the batteries and the bulb. Beyond that, the fewer such openings the better. Some lights have two O-rings at each opening for extra seal reliability. Regardless, you must maintain O-rings properly to ensure watertightness (more about this later).

Comfortable handle/mount

You can divide dive light handles into pistol grip, lantern grip and torch styles, with a few models that feature interchangeable grips. Let your preference

A dive light must have at least one watertight O-ring sealed opening that gives you access to the batteries and the bulb.

guide your choice, but don't underestimate its importance. Shallow night dives can last an hour or longer, so be sure to choose a grip that you find comfortable.

As a rule of thumb, most divers prefer a lantern grip on negatively buoyant lights, but a pistol grip on positively buoyant lights. Small lights, like most back-ups, are torch style.

Some small lights mount on your mask or hose, or other locations

Dive light handles are either pistol grip, (above) or lantern grip or torch style (right). Some models have interchangeable grips.

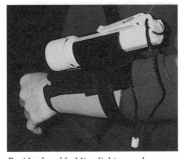

for hands free night diving. You can attach lights to camera strobes (which helps you aim) or other accessory equipment. If you mount your light on your mask, be sure it doesn't cause your mask to leak, and aim it so it doesn't shine in your buddy's eyes when you look at him.

Besides hand holding lights, you have mounting options too.

Lanyard

When you buy a dive light, if it doesn't come with a lanyard, get one for it. A lanyard helps you avoid accidental loss, and allows you to release the light when you need both hands for a moment. Most lanyards slip over your wrists, although you can purchase long, self-coiling lanyards that clip to your BCD.

While you want a lanyard that's secure, some are designed to stretch or fail under extreme load, such as if you snag your light while making a giant stride. This is a nice feature that can prevent injuries and light damage.

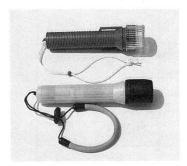

A lanyard helps you avoid accidental loss, and allows you to release the light when you need both hands for a moment.

Generally, you'll select a brighter light as your primary light and a more compact light as your backup.

Fresh/recharged batteries

A dive light's no better than its batteries. Before a dive be sure the batteries are fresh (disposable batteries) or fully charged (rechargeables). If there's doubt, replace/recharge them.

Choosing a Dive Light

Besides looking for the previous features, the dive light you choose depends on where you plan to use it, and the activities you plan to engage in. For example, in limited visibility many divers prefer a powerful, narrow beam. A very wide beam lights up all the suspended particles, creating a "fog" that's hard to see through. In clear water, wide beams don't have this problem, so they're useful to light as large an area as possible.

For looking into cracks and small areas, a narrow beam light works well. Also, for a given size and power, a narrow beam is brighter than wide beam. Many lights have a medium wide beam with a bright center; these make excellent lights for general application.

Special applications, like underwater videography, call for special lights. Video lights burn intensely and cannot be turned on out of water be-

Choosing a Dive Light

TYPE OF LIGHT BEAM

ACTIVITY		Narrow Beam/ Bright Spot	Medium Even Beam	Wide Even Beam	Wide Beam/ Bright Center Spot	Wide Beam/ Extremely Bright
NIGHT	Good Visibility	Poor	Good	Excellent	Excellent	Fair
	Low Visibility or Turbid Water	Good	Excellent	Good	Poor	Poor
	Checking gauges, spotlight for photography, etc.	Excellent	Good	Fair	Fair	Poor
	Underwater video	Poor	Poor	Fair	Fair	Excellent
	Pre- or Post-dive	Fair	Good	Excellent	Good	Poor
DAY	General Use	Good	Good	Good	Excellent	Fair
	Looking under ledges or in cracks and holes	Excellent	Good	Good	Excellent	Good

Light and Power

When you compare dive light specifications, understanding the terms manufacturers use simplifies your job. Most are straightforward, but not necessarily familiar to someone who doesn't work with lights routinely.

Candlepower/watts – A light's power/intensity is usually measured in watts, or less commonly, candlepower. A

A powerful rechargeable light will have a higher watt rating than a small backup light.

small backup light will be rated two to eight watts, a large primary 12 to 30 watts and a video light between 50 and 100 watts.

However, watts only tell part of the story; the light's reflector and bulb type affect the brightness. A wide beam light and a narrow beam light with the same power will have different brightness; the wide beam will cover a large area more dimly and the narrow a smaller area more brightly.

Although not as common in dive light specifications, brightness is measured in candlepower. Again, this is only part of the picture. A very narrow, low power light can have a higher candlepower than a high power, wide beam light.

In both instances, the

wattage or candlepower specified by the manufacturer generally assumes fresh batteries.

Lamps/bulbs – Light bulbs or lamps are rated by volts or amperes ("amps"). Volts rate the intensity of electrical power and amperes rate the quantity of power. The higher either rating is for a bulb, the greater a power source it needs.

For instance, a bulb for a powerful rechargable light may draw 1.2 amperes, while one for a disposable battery light draws .5. If the bulbs were switched, the rechargable batteries would quickly burn out the .5 bulb and the disposable batteries would lack sufficient power to light the 1.2 bulb.

Burn time/battery life – This describes the average time fresh batteries will last. Large bright lights usually have short burn times (one or two hours), while small lights may have five or six hour burn times. Burn time is an estimate, and varies depending on variations in bulb current requirement, and how you use the light — continuously or turned off and on. Use burn time to gauge approximate duration only.

Bulb life – The bulb life rating is based on how long 50 percent of test bulbs last. If a bulb has a 30 hour rating, that means that after 30 hours of use, 50 percent of the bulbs were still burning. In short, assuming no other damage, this means you have about a 50 percent chance of a bulb making it through its estimated life. Use bulb life ratings to compare how often you'll need to replace bulbs in various dive lights, but not to determine how long a particular bulb will last.

Bulb types – Bulbs are classified based on the gas in

them. Dive lights generally employ the whitest lights possible for the truest colors possible. Most dive lights are equipped with halogen or xenon gas bulbs, or a combination of both, which are among the whitest bulbs available.

Dive light bulbs contain gasses, such as halogen or xenon, which produce white light.

Halogen increases a bulbs wattage, extends its life and boosts its brightness, making it useful in high powered dive and video lights.

Halogen reduces the tungsten that vaporizes from the filament and blackens the bulb over time. Xenon bulbs come in lights of all sizes, and are brighter than krypton and argon bulbs, which are commonly used in surface lights.

Reflectors – Besides the bulb, reflector shape greatly affects a light's characteristics. The reflector concentrates or spreads the beam, for greater coverage with less over all brightness, or greater brightness but less over all coverage. A few models have adjustable bulbs and reflectors so you can vary the beam angle. Reflectors are fragile and easily scratched or marred when handled, so use caution when disassembling your light.

Reflectors concentrate or spread beams for greater coverage or greater brightness.

cause the heat will damage the light. With some models, the manufacturer advises removing or reversing the batteries when packing because if the light accidentally came on, it could start a fire. Check the manufacturer's guidelines to determine whether you can use a particular dive light out of water, especially if it is high powered.

Backup lights don't need to be as powerful as your primary light, but they need to provide adequate illumination to surface safely and exit the water. Backup lights work well for looking into holes and under ledges during the day, so you may want to choose one with that in mind, too.

Batteries

When choosing a dive light, you're also concerned with batteries: rechargeable or disposable. Both categories have different types, advantages, applications and maintenance considerations.

Disposable batteries include carbon zinc, alkaline and lithium batteries. Of these, carbon zinc, even the heavy duty type, is too underpowered for use in dive lights. Alkaline batteries are the most common disposables used in dive lights. You can get alkaline batteries in all the usual sizes for dive lights – C, D, AA, AAA, N or nine volt. You'll find lithium batteries used mainly in smaller lights.

Alkaline batteries have the advantage of a long burn time. As the batteries weaken, the light dims slowly, giving you adequate warning that you're getting low on power.

Lithium's primary advantage is that it has a long shelf life, making it a good choice for a backup light. Also, dive computers and digital gauges commonly use lithium batteries.

Disposable batteries have only a couple of maintenance considerations: If you're not going to use the light for an extended period, remove the batteries. When the batteries get weak, replace all the batteries with new, fresh batteries. Mixing weak and fresh batteries simply drains the new ones, and releases excess hydrogen.

Rechargeable batteries include rechargeable alkaline, nickel-cadmium (Nicad), nickel-hydride (Nihydride), lead-acid and gel-cell. Their character-

Rechargeable and disposable batteries have different advantages, applications and maintenance condiserations.

istics vary considerably.

Rechargeable alkalines are best used in smaller celled battery lights that usually take disposables, such as backups. Rechargeable alkalines perform much like disposable alkalines, but you can reuse them in standard lights up to approximately 25 times. However, due to the way they're made the larger C and D sizes don't hold as much power as a disposable alkaline; when used with high power dive lights, they may not be useful for the expected number of cycles.

In smaller AA and AAA sizes, there's little difference between rechargeable and disposable alkaline performance. This makes rechargeable alkalines suitable for smaller backup lights; another advantage is that unlike some other types of rechargeables, you can recharge one that's only partially discharged without affecting performance. This permits you to top up the batteries for the next dive without discharging them first.

By far, most rechargeable dive lights use nicads. Nicads include high capacity matched nicads and low resistance nicads, depending upon application. Regular dive lights usually employ high capacity nicads, and video lights usually employ low resistance, which stand up to heat better.

Nicads can power higher wattage bulbs and hold their power until they need recharging. This means your light will hold its brightness, then drop off quickly when you exhaust the batteries. All nicads (and other rechargeable batteries) cost more than disposables, yet they're less expensive in the long run —especially for the frequent night diver.

Most rechargeable batteries cost more than disposables, yet they're less expensive in the long run for the frequent night diver.

Nihydride batteries deliver more power than nicads, but you won't find them in dive lights (nor should you try to put them in one) because they put out a lot of hydrogen, which can be explosive in a sealed light.

Lead-acid and gel-cell batteries are found in some high intensity video lights. They can drive high powered bulbs, but they require special care and tend to be heavy.

Rechargeable batteries have specific maintenance requirements that you need to follow to get full performance and life expectancy from them.

If you travel, be careful to recharge your batteries using the proper current – an adapter kit may be needed.

They should be handled carefully, because dropping them can damage them so they no longer hold a charge. Most batteries should be allowed to cool before use after charging. Avoid discharging the batteries too deeply, which will cause them not to accept a charge. When the light gets very dim, turn it off and recharge them. If you travel internationally, be careful to recharge using the proper current; the wrong current can ruin your batteries instantly.

Nicads should not be recharged after a partial discharge. They should be discharged until the light gets dim, then recharged. If you partially discharge and recharge nicads repeatedly, they develop a "memory" and will only hold a partial charge. Some nicads have more trouble with memory than others, and most other rechargeables don't have this problem. Always follow the manufacturer's recommendations to assure optimum battery life.

With reasonable care, your rechargeable batteries will perform consistently for a long time. See your PADI Dive Center for information and options in rechargeable battery systems for dive lights. When choosing a light, if you want a rechargeable system, select a light designed for rechargeable batteries, and use on the batteries recommended by the manufacturer. With the exception of the rechargeable alkalines (which are really "rechargeable disposables"), don't put rechargeable batteries in a disposable battery light or vice versa.

Exercise 4   Underwater Light Systems

1. It's recommended that you night dive with at least _____ dive lights.
   - ☐ a. 1   ☐ b. 2   ☐ c. 3   ☐ d. 7

2. Which of the following features should you look for in a dive light (check all that apply)?
   - ☐ a. fresh batteries   ☐ b. lanyard   ☐ c. reliable switch   ☐ d. rugged case

3. Some high intensity dive lights shouldn't be turned on out of water because
   - ☐ a. the bulbs generate so much heat that without water cooling, the light will be damaged.
   - ☐ b. the lights are so bright they will drain the batteries, causing failure during the dive.

4. Dive lights with rechargeable batteries (check all that apply):
   - ☐ a. cost less to use in the long run for frequent night dives
   - ☐ b. require more care than disposable batteries
   - ☐ c. are not considered reliable
   - ☐ d. can power brighter bulbs than disposable batteries

How did you do?
1. b.   2. a, b, c, d.   3. a.   4. a, b, d..

Study Objectives

Underline/highlight the answers to these questions as you read:

1. How do you maintain a dive light?

2. How do you care for a flooded light?

Dive Light Maintenance

Like any dive equipment, your dive light requires proper care if you expect it to last and perform reliably. Proper maintenance begins immediately upon exiting the water.

You should rinse your dive light in fresh water as soon as possible after use, particularly if you've been diving in salt water or heavily chlorinated water. Ideally, rinse the light before it dries, which would leave a tough salt or chemical residue on it. If you can't get the light into fresh water immediately, it may be better to leave it in salt water until you can, or seal it in a bag so it doesn't dry out. This is important, because once salt dries, it forms sharp crystals that abrade O-rings. It can also be difficult to remove from recessed areas on the light, even with long soaks in fresh water.

Rinse your light in fresh water by swishing it back and forth for a minute or more.

Rinse the light in a freshwater bath, swishing it back and forth for a minute or so to flush out salt and particles from around switches and O-rings. Next, dry the light, open it and remove the batteries according to the manufacturer's instructions.

Inspect the battery contacts and clean them, if necessary, with a pencil eraser. After this, remove the O-rings and inspect them for nicks, cuts or wear. Replace worn or damaged O-rings.

Clean each O-ring gently with a lint free cloth, and clean the O-ring groove with cloth or a cotton swab. Inspect both the O-ring and the groove to be sure they're free of lint, hair or any debris that could cause a leak. Lubricate each O-ring with a small dab of silicone grease and distribute it evenly. Don't over lubricate – if done properly, the O-ring will appear shiny and wet, with no globs of grease visible. Reas-

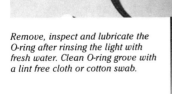

Remove, inspect and lubricate the O-ring after rinsing the light with fresh water. Clean O-ring grove with a lint free cloth or cotton swab.

semble the light and store it in a cool, dry place out of direct sunlight. If you won't be using the light for an extended period, disassemble the light and remove the O-rings. Store the O-rings, disassembled light and batteries in separate plastic bags.

How to Remove an O-ring

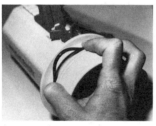

It's best to use only your fingers to remove the O-ring. If necessary, use the blunt corner of a certification card.

Once it's time to remove an O-ring, two points are critical: 1) Don't damage the O-ring, and 2) don't damage the O-ring groove. These easiest way to meet these objectives is to use *no tools*.

To do this, put your forefinger and thumb on the O-ring on opposite sides of the light. Push both your finger and thumb firmly toward each other along the O-ring, maintaining tension. Doing this causes the O-ring to stretch slightly, then bulge from its groove. Grasp the O-ring bulge with your other hand, then gently put your forefinger under it and trace around the groove to free it.

This will remove most O-rings with little chance of damage to it or the light. If you encounter one that's too tight and won't stretch, you'll need to use a tool. The safest tool is the blunt

corner of a credit card. Carefully work the corner under the O-ring to lift it from its groove. Once lifted, put your finger under it and lift it from its groove as before.

You may have seen a regulator technician at your dive store using a dental pick or another metal tool to extract small O-rings. Doing this requires experience and care, because metal tools can damage not only the O-ring, but the O-ring groove. If the groove is damaged, the light is ruined (an O-ring at least can be replaced) because it will not seal. Therefore, it's recommended that you avoid using anything other than your fingers or a credit card corner to remove O-rings. If you encounter a really stubborn O-ring, take it to your PADI Dive Center for removal.

Flooded Dive Lights

While you don't commonly flood dive lights, it does happen and by knowing what steps to take, you may minimize the damage to your light. Usually, you'll be underwater when you discover that your light has flooded. In fact, your buddy may notice first because lights don't necessarily go out immediately when they flood.

Immediately turn it off and switch to your backup light. When you exit the water, open the light very carefully, away from other people. Wet

If a light is flooded, open it very carefully away from other people, pour out the water and rinse thoroughly with fresh water.

batteries emit gas that can make the light pop apart or burst. If you can't attend to the light right away when you surface, put it someplace away from people where it won't cause damage if it pops apart on its own.

After you open the light, pour out the water, which will probably be contaminated with caustic chemicals. Avoid touching this water, and rinse thoroughly with fresh water if you do.

Dispose the batteries (unless the manufacturer says otherwise with rechargeables – if in doubt, discard them). Remember, wet batteries can very caustic; proper disposal is necessary to avoid health and/or environmental risks. Next, rinse the interior and exterior thoroughly with fresh water, the dry the interior with a hair dryer on the cool setting.

After flooding, your light needs to be serviced by a PADI Dive Center or the manufacturer. Some may be self-servicable, and in either case, you may have to have parts ordered. The reason is that many lights have a platinum catalyst that absorbs hydrogen gas released by the batteries. This catalyst is damaged by water and must be replaced to avoid dangerous gas buildups in the light.

Exercise 5

Dive Light Maintenance

1. After use, a dive light should be (check all that apply):
   - ☐ a. rinsed and soaked in fresh water
   - ☐ b. opened to inspect the batteries, electrical contacts and to maintain the O-rings
   - ☐ c. rinsed internally with alcohol
2. If a light floods, you should properly discard the batteries, rinse the interior with fresh water and have it serviced.　☐ True　☐ False

How did you do?
1. a,b.　2. True.

Study Objectives

Underline/highlight the answers to these questions as you read:

1. What are three uses for chemical lights or marker lights?

2. Where should you attach chemical lights or marker lights?

3. How can underwater strobes be used?

4. What are two uses for surface support lights?

By attaching a chemical or marker light to your tank valve, you can be seen more easily from the rear.

Lights for Navigation and Orientation

Besides your primary and backup lights, you'll find several other lights useful for night diving. These include chemical, marker, strobe and surface support lights. You use these for orientation to your entry/exit point, your buddy, and other locations. With these lights, you'll find night diving easier and more fun.

Chemical Lights and Marker Lights

Chemical lights (also known as "cyalumes" after the brand by that name and "glow sticks") and marker lights are small lights that can be applied three basic ways to help you and your buddy remain oriented. Chemical lights glow based on a chemical reaction; marker lights are small dive lights that run on disposable batteries.

First, they can mark each diver, even with dive lights turned off. Normally, you attach the chemical or marker light to your snorkel or tank valve, so you can be seen more easily from the rear.

Second, you can secure chemical or marker lights to the dive boat or your surface float so you can spot it easier when you surface. It also alerts boaters to your presence. Try to attach the light about three feet/one metre up on the flag staff.

Third, you can mark your ascent/descent line or anchor line with them so you can locate it easily. Some divers

Securing a chemical or marker light to your surface float makes it more visible.

like to attach several along its length, with a different color at 15 feet/5 metres to mark the safety stop depth.

You can get various attachments to secure them, or use rubber bands, tape, string or cable ties. It's important to attach them securely so they don't come loose and litter the reef or beach.

Chemical Light or Marker Light?

Ｎew night divers often ask which is better – disposable chemical lights or battery-powered marker lights? Each has its advantages and disadvantages.

Chemical lights contain two vials with chemicals. To activate the light, you bend the stick to break an inner vial and mix the chemicals. This starts a glowing reaction.

The advantage of a chemical light is that it doesn't depend on batteries or bulbs; there's nothing to wear out. Once lit, it stays lit for several hours. With a chemical light, you know you have at least one light that will be working, even if every other light you have fails (however unlikely).

The disadvantage of chemical lights is that you can't reuse them, and they're perishable. If you night dive regularly, it costs more to use chemical lights than marker lights, and you can't rely on old ones.

Marker lights are actually miniature dive lights, with a colored cone that glows, giving it the appearance of a chemical light. The primary advantage of marker lights is that they can be more economical to use than chemical lights.

The disadvantage is that because marker lights are miniature dive lights, they require the same care and lack the reliability of a chemical light. Their bulbs can burn out, they can flood, and their batteries can run down.

Ｂecause you throw chemical lights away after use, it's easy to think marker lights are more environmentally sound. Actually, since you throw away marker light batteries, both affect the environment. The important point is that used chemical lights and spent batteries should be disposed properly.

Strobe Lights

To spot your float, reference line or the boat from a long distance underwater, use a submersible strobe light (also known as "emergency flasher"). Strobe lights produce high intensity flashes at short inter-

vals, making them visible much farther away than chemical or marker lights. In clear water, you can see some models for 100 feet/30 metres or farther. In limited visibility, you can use the glow to remain oriented and near your exit.

Besides underwater use, you can put strobes on

the boat or float for easy identification at the surface. Some divers carry small strobes as emergency signals, too.

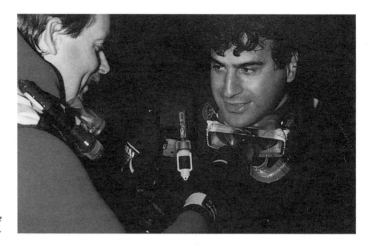

A diver may carry a small strobe to use as an emergency signal.

Surface Support Lights

Along with your dive lights, you'll want several surface lights when you night dive. You'll use surface lights to put your equipment on and, after the dive, take it off without draining your dive light batteries. They also help orient your entries and exits.

When you dive from a charter boat, the boat's lights usually provide adequate support. You can suit up by the deck lights, and at the end of the dive, the boat typically has several lights on, so you can locate it easily.

A charter boat's lights usually provide adequate support for suiting up.

When diving from shore, bring an area light or lantern to use a surface support.

To exit following a precise course, align two lights with your exit line – one high and to the rear, one close to the water.

After dark, before the dive, turn the lights on. If no one will attend your shore lights, leave a note explaining that they shouldn't be moved.

From small boats, you'll usually need some lights to gear up by. Also, be sure to mark the boat with at least a couple of lights so you can relocate it easily in the dark.

In most areas, local laws require boats at anchor to display navigation lights, regardless of size. Be sure to follow any such regulations.

When you dive from shore, you usually need to bring lights, although some docks and public beaches are well lit. For gearing up, choose an area light or lantern. Where possible, put an area light or lantern near your entry/exit point to help you get in and out of the water.

You may also need to mark your shore exit so you can find it at the end of the dive. Often, permanent lights such as streetlights or sign lights provide all the orientation you need; don't depend on lights that can be turned off, such as lights coming from a house or apartment. When you don't have permanent lights you can rely on, put a conspicuous light at your exit point. Ideally, leave someone ashore who can keep an eye on it (in case it burns out, for example). When you don't have someone on shore, leave a note on the light explaining that it's in use by divers and that it shouldn't be moved.

If you need to exit following a precise line, such as through a narrow cut in a rock reef or to avoid obstructions, you'll need two shore lights, preferably colored/flashing types distinct from any other lights visible on shore. Align the lights with your exit line, one high and to the rear, the other low and close to the water. The farther apart you get them, the more accurately they'll guide you in.

To follow your lights in after you surface, swim until you reach the point where they're aligned, then swim toward them. This should take you to shore along your desired path.

An important final point about shore lights — especially colored and flashing ones: Check local boat navigation lights and be sure that your lights won't confuse boaters.

Aquatic Life and Support Lights

Just as a dive light may attract aquatic organisms, so will support lights. Actually, support lights attract *more* life because they're usually very bright and remain in one place for a long period.

It's fun when your support lights attract schools of bait fish, squid and other interesting animals. On the other hand, they may also attract stinging creatures, particularly box jellyfish (sea wasps), which have a potent sting and pose a real hazard.

To minimize the problem, first check with local divers to find out what creatures may be attracted to support lights. If there's a possibility that a stinging animal would be among them, don't turn on support lights near the water until the last possible moment. This reduces the time the light draws in animals. In some instances, you may be able to have someone turn the light off until you return.

It may also help to plan your dives so you avoid long surface swims. Jellyfish tend to remain closer to the surface. Keep an eye on where you're going, and remember that an exposure suit, especially with a tucked-in hood, can reduce the likelihood of stings if you do encounter a jellyfish. Don't linger in the entry/exit area. Descend as soon as possible when you enter, and exit the water as soon as possible after your surface.

One technique is to plan your dive to have an extra large reserve. As you ascend, starting at about 20 feet/6 metres, hold down the purge button on your alternate second stage to start an air stream to the surface. This helps clear the ascent area of jellyfish and other floating organisms. Finally, if you might encounter stinging organisms in your dive environment, you may want to add sea sting treatment (commercially made ointments and vinegar) to your first aid kit.

Exercise 6

Lights for Navigation and Orientation

1. Chemical or marker lights are commonly used to mark the location of (check all that apply):
   - ☐ a. you and your buddy
   - ☐ b. surface floats
   - ☐ c. points of interest on the reef
   - ☐ d. ascent/descent lines

2. Chemical or marker lights may be attached
   - ☐ a. on a tank valve or snorkel
   - ☐ b. about three feet/one metre up on the surface float flag staff
   - ☐ c. on stag horn coral, kelp fronds or rock
   - ☐ d. along the length of the ascent/descent line

3. An underwater strobe should only be attached to the boat's anchor line. ☐ True ☐ False

4. Surface support lights (check all that apply):
   - ☐ a. assist you in gearing up and taking your gear off.
   - ☐ b. keep you oriented to your entry/exit points.
   - ☐ c. should not be used because they affect night vision.

How did you do?
1. a,b,d. 2. a,b,d. (c. is incorrect for both Question 1 and 2 because you don't want to attach lights to dive environment.) 3. False. You can use the strobe to mark reference lines, exit points, floats or as an emergency signal. 4. a,b. (c. is incorrect because surface lights affect your night vision no more than do dive lights.)

Study Objectives

Underline/highlight the answers to these questions as you read:

1. What should you consider when evaluating and choosing a night dive site?

2. What five environmental conditions should you try to avoid when planning a night dive?

3. What are the four general night dive planning recommendations?

Planning Night Dives

Planning night dives differs little from planning day dives. You need to choose an appropriate site, evaluate the conditions and prepare yourself and your equipment for the dive. The only difference is that you do each with the particular requirements of night diving in mind.

Choosing a Dive Site

Because it's easier to get disoriented at night, if possible choose a spot you're familiar with when you night dive. Even better, dive or snorkel the site during the day before your night dive.

By choosing a familiar site, you'll be acquainted with the site's layout, and know what visibility, surge, currents, surf, temperature and other conditions to expect. If you can snorkel/dive the site during the day, note specific spots you'd like to

After snorkeling or diving a site during the day, note specific spots to visit at night.

visit, and check the conditions. If you're shore diving, give particular attention to your entry and exit points.

When you can't day dive the site beforehand, consult your log book as necessary to reacquaint yourself with depths, topography and other features. Try to arrive before dark so you can look the site over and evaluate conditions.

As a general recommendation, it's preferable to avoid diving in an unfamiliar site at night. Rather, become familiar with the site during the day, then night dive there.

Although this is the best general recommenda-

The general recommendation is to avoid diving in an unfamiliar site at night.

tion, under a few circumstances it may be acceptable to night dive at an unfamiliar site. Under ideal conditions in a type of environment you're familiar with, you may find it acceptable, even though you've never been on that site before. For example, if you've been diving all week on coral reefs around an island in clear, currentless water, a night dive on a part of the reef you haven't seen would probably be acceptable. You may never have seen that exact coral head, but provided you evaluate the site and can locate your planned entrance and exit points, you'd be adequately familiar with the environment to have a fun, safe night dive.

Another such circumstance would be if you make the night dive with a professional dive guide or instructor who is familiar with the site. Visit a PADI Dive Center or Resort and ask about their Discover Local Diving night experiences.

If in doubt about whether it's appropriate to make a night dive at an unfamiliar site, of course stick with the general recommendation. Choose a familiar site for your dive.

Discover Local Diving

As you're probably aware, a diver of any certification level benefits from an area orientation when he dives in an unfamiliar area. The PADI Discover Local Diving experience provides an appropriate, supervised open water orientation to a new area.

During Discover Local Diving, you'll be guided by a PADI Divemaster, Assistant Instructor or Instructor who will brief you on local conditions, potential hazards, aquatic life, points of interest and special procedures used in the area. During the dive, he'll show you interesting points and what to avoid. Discover Local Diving doesn't include any specific skill evaluations, but rather helps you apply your skills in the local environment. On a night Discover Local Diving, you may review light use and other night procedures, too.

After the dive, you'll debrief about what you saw and the procedures you used. The PADI professional who conducted the experience will sign your log book, and he may also stamp it with a Discover Local Diving stamp.

Evaluating Conditions

You learned how to evaluate conditions during your entry-level scuba course; aside from having to use your dive light (if it's already dark), evaluating conditions for a night dive doesn't differ from any other dive.

What does differ, however, is where you draw the line between "acceptable" and "unacceptable" conditions. Primarily, you want conditions for a night dive to be a bit better than the worst conditions you would consider acceptable for a day dive. In particular, you want to avoid these:

Moderate to high surf

You may be adept at handling surf, but you may not realize it's much harder at night when you can't see the waves coming. Even smaller waves can knock you off your feet if they catch you by surprise, and in any case, it's difficult at best to judge changes in the surf at night. When the surf is marginal, it's probably best to cancel the dive or make a boat dive.

Moderate to strong currents

It's more challenging to navigate at night, and

When evaluating conditions for a night dive, you want them a bit better than the worst conditions you consider acceptable for a day dive.

Moonlit and Moonless Dives

Just as the underwater world differs between day and night, it differs between moonlit and moonless conditions. You'll find it makes a difference in your night dives, too.

When the moon shines brightly and you are diving in clear water, you may be surprised how well you can see underwater without your lights. Turn off or cover your light and let your eyes adjust. In a few moments, you'll be able to see your surroundings surprisingly well.

You may now see creatures that have shied from your dive light begin to emerge. However, predators see better in the moonlight, too, so most will stay close to shelter.

When it's moonless, or when you're diving in lower visibility so moonlight doesn't reach the bottom, you can't see much without your light. Notwithstanding, you may see a lot; usually more animals come out because they're less vulnerable to predators. In fact, some species – especially mollusks – emerge chiefly during the darkest phases of the lunar cycle.

currents complicate navigation to the point that it may be unreliable. If you're thrown off course and end up down current, you may not be able to reach your exit point, and when boat diving, you may be hard to spot for pick up. Consult the tide tables and check for currents when you evaluate conditions; if you find anything more than a light current, cancel the dive or move to a location out of the current.

Bad visibility

Assigning "good" versus "bad" to the visibility depends on the dive site. Nonetheless, visibility that complicates navigation unnecessarily, or reduces the possibility of seeing anything interesting, may be a good reason to cancel the dive.

Thick kelp, fishing nets, or anything that can entangle

With restricted visibility at night, it's harder to avoid potential entanglement. For that reason, keep well clear of such areas.

Heavy surge

Although most divers can manage surge during the day, at night surge can swing you into something before you see it. Surge can cause momentary vertigo during the day; night exacerbates this, making disorientation and vertigo likely. If you note heavy surge when you evaluate conditions, it's usually best to cancel diving.

Overhead environments

As mentioned earlier, even if you're equipped and trained for overhead environments, you should stay outside them at night.

General Night Dive Planning Recommendations

Once you've found a suitable night dive site, there are four recommendations that make night diving easier and more fun:

Prepare your equipment in daylight

Even when you have an area light or lantern, it's easier to set up your equipment while it's still light

If possible, prepare your equipment and make sure everything works before it gets dark.

out. Check it over to be sure everything works, particularly your dive lights. If you find you need to get new batteries (or recharge them), you may have ample time to do so. Go ahead and secure chemical or marker lights, too, but of course don't activate them until you're about to get in the water.

Eat a few hours before the dive

Diving properly fed makes a surprising difference on your comfort. Your body burns a lot of energy keeping warm, and especially if you've made a couple of dives earlier, your body's immediate energy reserves may be low. A proper, balanced meal assists in having the energy you need to stay warmer. In addition, drink plenty of noncaffeinated, nonalcoholic beverages to stay hydrated.

Dive with familiar buddies

Just as you night dive with familiar equipment so you can work with it instinctively, you want to dive with someone who you can interact with instinctively. Knowing your buddy's abilities and limits, and he yours, assures that you dive within both your limits.

Naturally, there are some reasonable exceptions. For example, if you were paired with a professional divemaster who's familiar with the environment, you don't have to be concerned with his ability as a night diving buddy. Be sure, though, to tell him about your skill and experience levels when you plan your dive.

It's convenient to have an extra hand when you get in and out of the water.

Bring a friend

Whether diving from boat or shore, it's convenient to have an extra hand getting in and out of the water. A friend who isn't making the dive can tend lights, hand or take accessories from you, and provide assistance in an emergency. Charter boats usually have someone aboard to do this, which is one reason many divers prefer night diving from charter boats.

Exercise 7

Planning Night Dives

1. When choosing a site for a night dive, you want to consider (check all that apply):
    ☐ a. topography ☐ b. conditions ☐ c. entry/exit point
2. Environmental conditions you should avoid when night diving include (check all that apply):
    ☐ a. heavy surf ☐ b. surge ☐ c. thermoclines ☐ d. sources of entanglement
3. It's a good idea to bring someone to stay at the surface on a night dive to tend support lights and lend assistance. ☐ True ☐ False

How did you do?
1. a,b,c. 2. a,b,d. (c. is incorrect because thermoclines require a proper exposure suit, but aren't a reason to call off night dives) 3. True

Study Objectives

Underline/highlight the answers to these questions as you read:

1. How can you minimize and cope with stress during a night dive?

2. What should you do if your light fails during a night dive?

3. What should you do if you become separated from your buddy during a night dive?

4. What should you do if you become disoriented or lost during a night dive?

Special Night Diving Situations

Night Diving Stress

Most divers experience a bit of mental stress when they first enter the water on a night dive. If you have yet to try your first night dive, you may be surprised to learn that heightened excitement produces some of the fun.

Humans – and most animals – instinctively fear the unknown. When someone faces an unfamiliar situation, this fear may range from caution to alarm and panic, depending upon how much threat the individual perceives or imagines. On a night dive, even in a familiar site, darkness conceals the underwater world until you put your light on it. Instinctively, you become a bit more cautious, but to a degree that makes night diving exciting and adventurous. As you become familiar with your surroundings, you relax.

However, too much stress takes the fun out of night diving. This can happen if you imagine unreal, irrational hazards, which leads to fear/stress with no basis. Or, if you encounter an actual potential hazard unexpectedly, you'll feel fear and/or high stress.

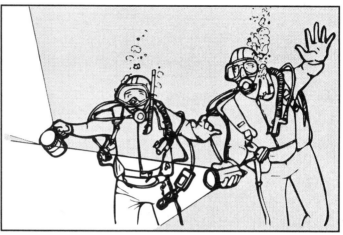

A little stress while night diving is normal; your goal is to manage stress so that it contributes to your fun and excitement.

Fortunately, you can easily minimize and cope with "fear of the unknown;" your weapon is knowledge. By reading this book, watching the PADI *Night Diving* video and completing the PADI Night Diver course and/or Advanced core night dive, you gain knowledge and skills that displace irrational fears, and reduce the probability of encountering a significant hazard on a night dive. Knowing that you'll make some of your first night dives with an experienced PADI Instructor should also boost your confidence and reduce stress.

As you become an experienced night diver, keep a few tips in mind to help keep stress in check. Evaluate conditions as described in the previous section, and don't dive in adverse ones. Avoid trying to do too much on a night dive, or trying to go too far. Plan night dives for a relaxed pace. Be sure you've adjusted your equipment so it's comfortable and you can work it by touch.

If you do encounter a problem on a night dive, stop, think and then act, just as you would on a day dive. Stopping and breathing deeply and regularly mentally shifts you away from instinctive reactions toward rational thought and proper action.

If your primary light fails, switch to your backup, signal your buddy and ascend.

Light Failure

There are a few problems specific to night diving, including light failure. If your light fails, simply stop, switch to your backup and signal your buddy. At this point, you and your buddy should head for the boat or shore; don't continue a night dive on your backup.

In the rare instance that your backup doesn't work (or was lost), signal your buddy and borrow his backup. In the very unlikely circumstance that his doesn't work either, leaving the two of you with only one light, ascend together immediately, conditions allowing. By doing this, you avoid the possibility of having to ascend with no light.

Having to ascend without a light would mean that either you and your buddy had a quadruple light failure/light loss, or that you separated from your buddy and had a double light failure/light loss. However unlikely, you can still make a slow, safe ascent without a light if necessary.

First, take a moment to let your eyes adjust – you may be able to see more than you realized without a light. If you're near a reference line, use it to guide and control your ascent. A line marked with chemical or marker lights works even better.

Without a line, use your gauges for reference. You'll be able to read glowing or lit gauges; with other gauges, try using a chemical or marker light.

If you're with your buddy, make contact and ascend slowly, one hand up to avoid obstacles, watching your gauges. Maintain a rate of 60 feet/18 metres per minute or slower, or as specified by your dive computer. If you become disoriented, look at your bubbles to reorient you to up and down. Conditions allowing, hover at 15 feet/5 metres and make a three minute safety stop.

Buddy Separation

In some ways, it's easier to keep track of your buddy at night than during the day. During the day, you have to keep turning to look for him; at night, as long as his light beam illuminates a path near yours, you know he's there. You'll want to communicate with him regularly, of course, but this simplifies staying together.

If you lose your buddy, stop, shine your light down and away, and look for the glow of your buddy's light.

Even with good communication, though, you may become separated. As soon as you notice, stop, shine your light down and away from you, and look for the glow of your buddy's light. If you don't see it, rise slightly and cover your light. Rotate in place, looking up and down for the faint glow of his light. If you still don't see it, shine your light straight out from you and rotate, so that perhaps your buddy will find you.

If this doesn't get you and your buddy together, follow standard procedure: Look for no more than a minute, then surface slowly and regroup on the surface.

When planning your dive, it's good idea for you and your buddy to discuss what to do if separated. Agreeing on your course and keeping track of each other will reduce the chance separation in the first place.

Disorientation

Recommended night diving techniques help minimize disorientation problems. Descending/ascending with a reference, and choosing a familiar dive site, for example, go a long way in keeping you oriented to your surroundings.

Sometimes, however, you may become disoriented or suffer vertigo in midwater during descent. If you're near a reference line, hold on to it until your orientation returns. Without a reference line, hold on to your buddy or hug yourself, and watch

If you and your buddy are disoriented on the bottom, consult your compass to determine which way you are facing relative to the boat or shore.

your bubbles. Once you have your bearings, disorientation should pass. If not, surface slowly and discontinue the dive. On occasion, you may lose your way on the bottom. If you and your buddy discover that you don't know where you are, stop. Consult your compass to determine which way you're facing relative to the boat or shore. Look around for natural navigation clues, such as the edge of a reef or jetty or a familiar landmark. Reestablish your location before moving on.

If these steps don't reorient you, surface carefully with your buddy and check your position. Time and air allowing, you may redescend and continue your dive.

Exercise 8

Special Night Diving Situations

1. Knowing and applying appropriate night diving procedures is an important step in controlling stress. ☐ True ☐ False
2. If your primary light fails during a dive ☐ a. switch to your backup and continue the dive. ☐ b. switch to your backup and end the dive. ☐ c. ascend slowly and carefully.
3. If you and your buddy become separated, shine your light down and away from you, and rotate looking for the glow of his light. ☐ True ☐ False
4. If you become disoriented on a night dive (check all that apply):
   ☐ a. keep swimming in the direction you're headed.
   ☐ b. consult your compass for your relative heading.
   ☐ c. look for familiar landmarks.
   ☐ d. surface if necessary to reestablish your location.

How did you do?
1. True.   2. b, (a. is incorrect because you shouldn't continue the dive on a backup; c. is incorrect because you should have a backup)   3. True.   4. b,c,d.

When entering at night, check the entry with your lights and enter as you normally would.

Night Diving Techniques

By now it's pretty clear that most techniques and procedures unique to night diving revolve around dive light use. You'll find this especially true for night entries, exits, ascents, descents and communication. By reviewing the PADI *Night Diving* video, you can see the following techniques in use:

Entries and Exits

After evaluating conditions, planning your dive, gearing up and making your predive safety check, you're ready to enter the water. If you're diving from a boat:

- Turn on your primary light and put the lanyard around your wrist. This keeps you from losing it if you accidentally drop it, and makes it easy to find if it comes off your wrist.
- Check the entry area with your light.
- Enter as you normally would.
- Signal "okay" and clear the entry area. Don't shine your light up to the boat, which can blind those aboard.

If you're diving from shore:

- Turn on your primary light and put the lanyard around your wrist. This keeps you from losing it if you accidentally drop it, and makes it easy to find if it comes off your wrist.
- Check the entry area with your light for rocks or obstructions.
- If you're entering through light surf, time your entry for a lull in the waves. Watch for waves frequently with your light as you enter.
- Enter as you normally would.
- Stay close to your buddy, and be careful not to shine your light in his eyes.

When exiting, use similar techniques: Turn your light on so you can see, and in case you drop it.

Turn your light on when exiting so you can see, and in case you drop it.

Don't shine it in the boat or shore tender's eyes. When exiting through surf, time your exit for a lull and keep an eye out for waves as you go.

Descents and Ascents

A reference makes ascents and descents easier at night, just like during the day, especially in moderate visibility. If you're diving from shore, you can often use the bottom as your reference. If you're diving from a boat, or with a float, a reference/anchor line provides a good reference. In clear, shallow water, you may not need a reference.

Stay with your buddy when you descend along a line, adjusting your buoyancy so you reach the bottom neutrally buoyant. Use your light to watch ahead of you as you descend. Descend in a head-up position so you stay oriented.

When you ascend, use your depth gauge and the line to guide your ascent rate. Use your light to look upward and watch for obstructions. Remember to be a S.A.F.E. Diver – Slowly Ascend From Every Dive no faster than 60 feet/18 metres per minute, with a three-minute safety stop at 15 feet/5 metres.

While descending, stay with your buddy, adjust your buoyancy and use your light to watch ahead of you.

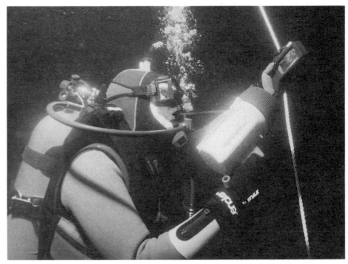

Ascending along a line, using your depth gauge or computer as a reference helps you maintain a proper rate.

Keep in mind that safety stops are as – if not more – important on a night dive as a day dive. If

Walls and Black Water Descents

In some instances, you may need to descend without a reference in water that's deeper than your light penetrates. During these descents, you need to watch your buddy and gauges closely.

When you're diving along a wall, pay particular attention to the depth. If you miss the wall, you could accidentally exceed your planned depth. If you reach the depth at which you should see the wall and don't, be prepared to reascend carefully, using gauges to track a safe ascent rate.

your night dive follows two or three day dives, the safety stop helps keep you within conservative nitrogen limits. Since it's harder to see references at night, the safety stop gives you a chance to get your buoyancy under control and avoid ascending too fast as you near the surface.

Marking the safety stop on your reference line makes maintaining stop depth easier in the dark. If you don't have a reference, use your buddy and depth gauge/dive computer to maintain your safety stop depth.

When you surface, inflate your BCD and signal "okay" to the boat or shore tender. If necessary, take a moment to rest before heading to your exit. You may find your way easier during surface swims with your light out.

Communication

You use the same hand signals at night as you do during the day, but you need to be sure your buddy can see them and that you don't blind him with your light in the process. First, get your buddy's attention by rapping on your tank, waving your light or gently touching him. Considering somewhat higher stress levels at night, don't suddenly grab or startle him.

When you have his attention, signal with your signaling hand low (waist level) and/or out to the side. Shine your light on your signal, pointing the light away from your buddy. If you need two hands

To communicate with hand signals, shine your light on your hand at waist level.

You can signal okay at the suface by holding your light so it points down on your head.

for the signal, have your buddy use his light, or use your slate instead. If you're a bit away from your buddy, swing your light in a big circle to indicate "okay."

At the surface, use the same signal to mean "okay." Also, you can signal "okay" by holding your light so it points down on your head. Signal "need assistance" by waving your light. If necessary, use your whistle to get the boat or shore tender's attention. Night diving light signals aren't universal, so it's a good idea to review them with your buddy and the boat crew before you dive.

Rapid Light Movement

A rapidly waving or jerky light beam alerts you to one of two things:

1. Someone wants your attention.

2. Someone's not holding or controlling his light, indicating a possible problem. In either case, you don't want to ignore it.

Whenever you notice rapid light movement, determine the source and cause.

Night Diving Courtesy

Night dives take place when other people may be going to bed, so give thought to common courtesy. If you're diving near residences or campsites, keep noise – clanking tanks and weights, regulator hiss and blowing your dust cap dry – to a minimum. Speak softly and keep your light off of windows, cars, boats, tents and out of people's eyes. In some areas, night diving has been banned because discourteous individuals bothered local residents.

In the water, be courteous of your buddy. Don't shine your light in his eyes; point at leg level when you're trying to identify or locate a diver.

A little forethought avoids ill will with divers and nondivers alike.

Exercise 9

Night Diving Techniques

1. When you enter the water at night, turn off your light so you don't accidentally blind someone.   ☐ True ☐ False
2. To reduce disorientation, it helps to ascend/descend   ☐ a. alone.   ☐ b. along a reference.   ☐ c. by compass.
3. When you signal at night, hold your hand to the side and at waist level.   ☐ True ☐ False

How did you do?
1. False. Leave your light on so you can find it if you lose it.   2. b.   3. True.

Study Objectives

Underline/highlight the answers to these questions as you read:

1. What are the procedures for relocating a dive site at night?

2. What natural navigation techniques do you use to avoid disorientation at night?

3. What compass navigation techniques do you use to avoid disorientation at night?

Night Diving Navigation

At night, the best navigation is the simplest. Reduce your pace, and don't try to go as far as you would during the day. By following a simple reciprocal course or a casual square, you can usually enjoy the night dive and remain oriented through out the dive.

Locating an Offshore Dive Site

When night diving from shore, you may want to visit a specific spot away from shore. A few techniques make finding the spot easier.

When possible, visit the spot earlier, either snorkeling or scuba diving. You may be able to leave a buoy or surface float to mark the spot. If not, note features in the area and the compass heading to and from your entry/exit point. Look at the relative location of above-water objects such as

Use a compass heading, along with above-water navigational aids, to relocate a dive site.

navigational buoys, rocks, piers and trees.

After dark, enter and allow your eyes to adjust. Swim on the surface following your compass; your buddy should follow and stay close to you. If the water's clear enough, use your light to look for familiar features on the bottom. Otherwise, check above-water landmarks; when you're in the vicinity, descend and navigate to your spot following bottom features.

Look for landmarks or features, like sand ripples or depth, that will help you navigate and keep you oriented.

Natural Navigation Techniques

Natural navigation relies on maintaining a mental picture of where you are at all times, based on features and navigation clues that surround you. For more precision, you can map your course on a slate to find your way back. Look for obvious landmarks and other distinct features that keep you oriented. Pay particular attention to these:

Water movement

Waves, surge or light current all provide a relative direction. Surge swings back and forth from shore, and currents flow in a single direction, although they can change. In rivers, springs or streams, the water flow remains constant.

Sand or mud ripples

Bottom ripples run parallel to shore, following the contour. If you swim perpendicular to ripples, you're either headed shoreward (usually getting shallower) or away from shore (usually getting deeper).

Rock/reef formation

Coral or rock reefs often form long natural lines. One of the easiest ways to navigate is to follow a reef edge out and back.

Depth

Note your depth relative to the bottom contour and your exit point. As you return, depth helps you judge how close you are to your exit.

Light

Especially in clear water, light – from the boat or shore, a strobe or along your reference line – helps you keep your bearings.

Compass Navigation Techniques

It's a good idea to wear a compass on any dive, but you'll find one especially useful at night because you can't observe your surroundings quite as readily.

Take a compass heading to your destination and to your exit before you descend. When you reach the bottom, this heading will guide you and help you stay oriented relative to your exit. If you'll be using multiple compass headings during the dive, you may want to note this heading on your slate.

Most of the time, you'll combine natural and compass navigation. Keep your navigation simple,

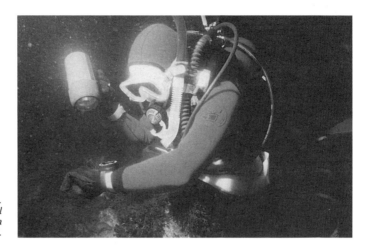

Keep your navigation simple. For example, follow a general compass heading out and return on the reciprocal.

especially for your first night dives. For example, you may follow a general compass heading out, away from the boat or shore, noting natural features as you go. You return on the reciprocal heading, using natural navigation to confirm your location.

In lower visibility, use several short courses. Starting, for instance, at the anchor line, follow a compass heading out and back a short distance. When you return to the anchor line, choose another heading and repeat the process. You can do this as long as you have ample air; the advantage is that you see a good deal, while remaining oriented and close to the boat.

Navigating to the Exit

When possible, plan night dives so that you return to your exit, or as close as possible, underwater. When diving from a boat or calm shore, this is usually feasible and avoids a more tiring surface swim.

It helps to plan your exit at the beginning of the dive, before you descend. Look back toward the boat or shore while you're still oriented and note

47

PADI Underwater Navigator Specialty Course

The PADI Underwater Navigator Specialty course improves your compass and natural navigation skills.

Few skills mark the accomplished diver as conspicuously as underwater navigation. No matter what type of dive you're making, the ability to navigate saves air and time, reduces stress and increases your fun.

The PADI Underwater Navigator Specialty course improves your compass and natural navigation skills. In it, you learn to relocate a dive site from the surface, how to make underwater maps, effectively use navigation patterns, use navigational tools and refine your natural/compass navigation.

The PADI *Underwater Navigator Manual* and *Underwater Navigation* video provide the knowledge foundation for this course, followed by practice on several training dives. Mastering underwater navigation not only gives you a practical skill, but it gives you the satisfaction of measuring up to a fun challenge.

For more information about the PADI Under water Navigator course, see your PADI Instructor or PADI Dive Center.

what your exit looks like from the water.

At the end of your dive, if you must return to your exit on the surface, cover your dive light and let your eyes adjust. Look for your boat or shore lights; if you have trouble spotting them, use your compass to show you which way to look. Swim slowly, take your time and watch for obstructions. Use your light to check the area as you exit.

Exercise 10

Night Diving Navigation

1. To relocate an offshore dive site while night diving (check all that apply):
   - ☐ a. use a compass heading you noted earlier.
   - ☐ b. use natural navigation aids you noted earlier.
   - ☐ c. use your light to illuminate features on the bottom.

2. Natural navigation features that may help you find your way include (check all that apply):
   - ☐ a. water movement   ☐ b. sand/mud ripples   ☐ c. visibility   ☐ d. depth

3. Navigating out and back on a reciprocal course with a compass is an effective night diving navigation technique.   ☐ True   ☐ False

How did you do?
1. a,b,c.   2. a,b,d (c. is incorrect because visibility gives no indication of direction)   3. True

Night diving may motivate you to learn more about nocturnal aquatic species, or take up underwater photography – the possibilities are endless.

Continuing Your Adventure

The techniques you read about here and practice in the PADI Night Diver Specialty course open the door to a new underwater world – the world of night. As your night diving experience grows, so will your confidence and curiosity.

As you night dive more often, you may feel motivated to take up underwater photography/videography, or learn more about nocturnal aquatic species – the possibilities are endless. With proper planning, you'll find all your night dives satisfying adventures.

Night Diver Specialty Course Training Dives Overview

The following outlines the three dives you'll make as part of your PADI Night Diver Specialty course. Your instructor may partially rearrange the sequence within each dive, or may add additional dives based on your needs and environmental conditions.

Note: During your training dives, you'll be using the Recreational Dive Planner, either Table or The Wheel. If you want to refresh yourself in using these, see the *Scuba Tune-up* guidebook or the *Diving With The Wheel* video.

Night Diver Training Dive One

- Knowledge Review
- Briefing
- Assemble surface and underwater lights
- Suiting Up
- Predive Safety Check (BWRAF)
- Entry – compass heading

- Descent
- Navigation exercise
- Tour
- Ascent – Safety Stop
- Debrief
- Log Dive

Night Diver Training Dive Two

- Briefing
- Assemble surface and underwater lights
- Suiting Up
- Predive Safety Check (BWRAF)
- Entry
- Descent
- Navigation exercise
- Tour – noting nocturnal aquatic life
- Ascent – Safety Stop
- Debrief
- Log Dive

Night Diver Training Dive Three

- Briefing
- Assemble surface and underwater lights
- Suiting Up
- Predive Safety Check (BWRAF)
- Entry – take compass heading
- Free descent
- Three-minute light out exercise
- Independent tour in buddy teams
- Ascent – Safety Stop
- Debrief
- Log Dive

Knowledge Review — Part I

Note to student: The first half of this Knowledge Review is the same Knowledge Review in the Night Diving section of *Adventures in Diving*. If your instructor has the first half on file from your PADI Advanced Open Water Diver or Advanced Plus course, he may, at his discretion, have you complete only the second half of this Knowledge Review.

Answer the following questions and bring this completed Knowledge Review with you to your next training session.

1. State the recommendation regarding the use of new or unfamiliar equipment on a night dive.

2. List three uses for chemical light sticks and where they are attached for those uses.

    1. _____

    2. _____

    3. _____

3. Describe what you will want to consider and evaluate in choosing a potential dive site for night diving.

4. What are the five environmental conditions you should avoid when night diving?

    1. _____

    2. _____

    3. _____

    4. _____

    5. _____

5. What are four general night diving planning considerations?

    1. _____

    2. _____

    3. _____

    4. _____

6. Briefly describe what you should do if you experience stress, light failure, buddy separation or disorientation while night diving.

    a. Stress:

    b. Light failure:

    c. Buddy separation:

    d. Disorientation:

7. Briefly describe the procedures for entering the water at night from a boat and from shore.

8. Describe the proper techniques for descending and ascending at night so as to avoid disorientation and undue stress.

9. List the methods of communication while night diving.

10. Briefly describe the navigational techniques used to avoid disorientation and loss of direction while night diving.

Knowledge Review — Part II

11.   State the rule regarding overhead environments and night dives.

12.   List night diving considerations that apply to your personal dive equipment.

13.   Explain why it's important to carry at least two dive lights on a night dive.

14.   Describe the advantages and disadvantages of rechargeable and nonrechargeable batteries in dive lights.

15.   Describe how to maintain a dive light.

16. Describe what to do if your dive light floods.

17. List three uses for chemical or marker lights.
    1. _____
    2. _____
    3. _____

18. Explain how underwater strobes can be used:

19. List two uses for surface support lights:
    1. _____
    2. _____

20. Describe how to be courteous while night diving.

Student Statement:

I have had explained to me and I understand the questions I missed.

Name _____ Date _____

PADI Student Transcript Request

Mail This Request To:
Office of Academic Transcripts
PADI International, Inc.
1251 E. Dyer Rd. #100, Santa Ana, CA 92705-5605

Personal Information – (Please Type or Print Clearly)

Student Name _____

Student Mailing Address_____

City _____State/Province _____

Country _____Zip Code _____

Phone (____) _____ FAX (____) _____

Birth Date _____ Sex ☐ M ☐ F Social Security Number _____ _____ _____

Transcript Mailing Information

☐ Self – *Mail _____ transcript(s) to address indicated in Personal Information section.*

☐ College or University – *One transcript will be sent to the institution listed below.*

Name of Institution _____

Address _____

City _____ State/Province _____

Country_____ Zip Code_____

Note: If you need transcripts sent to more than one institution, please include the names and addresses on an additional sheet of paper. All transcripts sent to a college or university are addressed to the Registrar's Office.

Transcript Fee

Please include $15 for the first transcript and $5 for each additional transcript ordered.

Payment Method

☐ I am requesting _____ transcript(s) at $15 for the first and $5 for each additional.

Total Enclosed $ _____

Check *(Must be payable to PADI International in U.S. Dollars, and drawn on a U.S. Bank.)*

☐ MasterCard ☐ VISA Card No. _____ _____ _____ _____

Expiration Date _____

Cardholder Name *(please print)*_____

Authorized Signature_____

Verification of Certification — Please Read Carefully

For **each** recognized PADI course you want to have listed on your transcript, you must submit proof of course completion by one of the two following methods: 1) include this form with either a PIC envelope or Divemaster Application, OR 2) attach a clear photocopy of the **front** and **back** of your certification card(s) or validation card(s) to this form.

Receive College Credit for PADI Diver-Training Courses

The American Council on Education (ACE) recommends college credit for certain PADI scuba diver courses. ACE represents all colleges and universities before the U.S. federal government and as such is the unified voice of higher education. ACE evaluates educational courses according to established college-level criteria and recommends college credit for those that measure up to these standards.

The ACE credit recommendations for PADI courses may help you in receiving college credit at an American university or college – *even if the courses aren't conducted on a university or college campus.* Courses offered through PADI Dive Centers, Resorts and other locations qualify.

Take a Course – Use the Credit

A university or college may use the ACE credit recommendations in a variety of ways. The institution may apply the credit to your major replacing a required course. They may also use the credit as a general elective to possibly waive a prerequisite course.

College Credit at No Extra Charge

Universities and colleges that accept ACE credit recommendations for PADI courses typically handle them like transfer credit. Transfer credit is often awarded without an additional fee. This may save you tuition fees while at the same time allowing you to possibly meet graduation requirements.

How Much College Credit Can I Earn?

ACE has set forth the following college credit recommendations for PADI Courses:

Course	Semester Credit Hours	Division*	Instructional Area
Open Water Diver	1	Lower	Recreation/Physical Education
Night Diver	1	Lower	Recreation/Physical Education
Advanced Open Water Diver and Advanced Plus	1	Lower	Recreation/Physical Education
Deep Diver	1	Lower	Recreation/Physical Education
Rescue Diver	1	Lower	Recreation/Physical Education
Divemaster	2	Lower	Recreation/Physical Education
IDC	2	Upper	Recreation/Physical Education or Education
Course Director Training Course	3	Upper	Recreation/Physical Education or Education

*Lower - Typically Freshman/Sophomore Level; Upper - Typically Junior/Senior Level

Ordering an Official PADI Transcript

To secure credit for a PADI course at a college or university you need an official transcript as proof of course completion. *Colleges and universities will not accept certification cards or wall certificates as proof of course completion.* PADI will send your transcript directly to you or the college or university you are currently attending or planning to attend. It is recommended that you also order a transcript for your own records. To order an official transcript, complete the application on the next page and enclose the indicated processing fee.